WINGS OF TIME

SELECTED POEMS

By

Aman B. Kay

Special thanks to Loretta Levi for her constant support and assistance in making valuable recommendations regarding my writing and her guidance in technical aspects of this manuscript.

Copyright © 2012 Aman B. Kay

All rights reserved

ISBN-10: 1475215258

ISBN-13: 978-1475215250

CreateSpace, North Charleston, SC

Cover photo by Sylvia L. Ramsey

Poet's photo by Susan Levi

JUST A LITTLE CHAT

Some of the verses in this collection have appeared in various periodicals like *Poet: An International Monthly; Ardent: A Journal of Poetry and Art; Jointure: Poets and Arts; Jane's Journal*, and many other American and international publications that are simply too numerous to be named here.

A poet can never express enough appreciation to so many men and women who have contributed to the creation and the writing of his/her verses over years and decades of direct and indirect support. To all of you who have been a constant inspirational and supportive force in my life, I can only extend a sincere poetic "thank you." I can only hope that I have made the proper connection by demonstrating the value and importance of each one of you in my life. If I were to name all of you, it would be merely too long of a list to be included in this little chat. I am truly hopeful that if you choose to read my verses, you will be able to identify your signature of friendship in and between selected lines. The cultural, emotional, logical, and literary impact of valuable relatives, friends, and colleagues on a poet is so vast and deep that only within his/her poems one can sense its presence.

*   *   *

In my early childhood mind, cancer had the form of a giant frightening monster: Grendel-like. It swallowed defenseless people for no reason. With no remorse. I have lost my beloved mother, some precious relatives, and a number of exceptional friends and colleagues to this monster. These days, though, the commendable dedication and the ongoing effort of scientists and all others who have directly and indirectly been involved in fighting against cancer, to a good degree, have contained this indiscriminating monster.

This collection of poetry is dedicated to these amazing men and women, to the memories of the victims, and to the resilience and courage of the survivors, THESE CHERISHED SOULS (p.72), who keep fighting as they teach us the beauty and value of every precious breath of life. I am delighted that 100% of the proceeds of this book will be directly contributed to the Winship Cancer Institute (WCI) at Emory University. I deeply and sincerely salute the dedication of all men and women who are working tirelessly to give humanity more practical tools and are generating much needed help in fighting the cancer-monster. We have come a long, glorious way and much better days can be realistically expected.

To catherine
All the best
Amy

"A hundred times every day I remind myself that my inner and outer life depends on the labors of other men, living and dead, and that I must exert myself in order to give in the measure as I have received and am still receiving."

—Albert Einstein

CONTENTS

POETS AND POETRY BENEATH THE WINGS OF TIME	9
PREFACE	19
WINGS OF TIME	20
TEMPORAL DOMICILE	25
THE BURNING	29
MIGRATION	31
NEDA'S ETERNAL CALL	33
REPLY	35
TO ALL THE NEGLECTED GIRLS	37
THE ANCIENT DREAM	39
ELEGY FOR A WANDRING SOUL	43
THE SONNET OF DISTANCE	46
LIFE	47
THE FALLING BIRD	49
THE ELEGY IN AUTUMN	52
THE LOST SOULS	53
TEARS AND CELEBRATION	56
COULD WE?	60
NO MAN'S LAND	61
DARK PASSAGE OF HUMANKIND	62
THAT MONSTROUS GOD	63
HENCE THE SEASON OF LIFE	65

THE FORBIDDEN LAND	68
THE BROKEN SPIRIT	69
THESE CHERISHED SOULS	72
WHERE ARE YOU?	75
THE SONG OF ALWAYS	77
THAT THING	79
SONGS BORN TO THE EARTH-MOMENTS	81
THE DIVINE EMBASSADOR OF ETERNAL RAINBOWS	87
THE DREAM THAT DREAMS	91
FOR WADE JOSEPH SMITH	94
EPILOGUE	98
ABOUT THE POET	100

POETS AND POETRY BENEATH
THE WINGS OF TIME

"Poets are shameless with their experiences: they exploit them." Thus spoke Friedrich Nietzsche. And thus the three questions embedded in this debatable statement by a brilliant but overly pessimistic nineteenth century philosopher: 1) Who is a poet? 2) What is really the meaning of the concept of "experience" and its relevancy to poetry? And 3) how does one "exploit" private matters by using fancy terms and poetic techniques? Who is a poet? Is a poet the person who composes/creates a verbal art that includes "love of wisdom," or is there more to a poet than a mere hunting for certain points in moments of selected occurrences? By expressing human's deep desires, dreams, hopes, ambitions, disappointments, and above all the delicate emotions that depict love and hate, most poets have been the truthful narrators of their era. They have documented history and developed universal themes that have brought humanity together. The tradition of poetry writing is so deep, so strong that it is an impossibility to believe that poets of various centuries have fabricated their experiences.

From *The New Princeton Encyclopedia of Poetry and Poetics* we learn that "The Hebrew Bible constituted the foundation and principal component of [literary] heritage" and the book is "a major source for literary forms, symbols, rhetorical tropes, syntactic structures, and vocabulary." Since from early times in human life poetry has emerged and has been kept alive by generation after generation in practically every culture, there is much to be said about the truthfulness that people recognized and celebrated in poetic expressions. True poets did not attempt to compete with religious beliefs nor did they impose their ideology. The majority remained the true narrators of their times, and a few agenda-driven selected poets, from each era, were gradually eliminated by future generations.

The vast majority of poetry readership realized that true poetry did not have an agenda. True poetry has never been in search of answers, solutions, guidance, or especially, redemption. True poetry has always been a journey. Like life. Like love. Like the thrill of being in love. Like salt water departing from the eyes as the sincere reaction to pain, to sorrow, to the inability to comprehend a situation, or the lack of capability to deal with it. The truthful narrators have cried tears of hopelessness and helplessness with, and for, humanity. It is then no wonder that primitive shepherds were the first poets, the first song writers, the first lonely souls who needed to refuse the mountainous presence of their physical, environmental, and spiritual loneliness. They did not seek, nor hope for, concrete, materialistic satisfaction. Rather, they looked for temporal refuge. And in their basic lyrics they explored gateways to the comfort of expression and further emotional need for communicating their hidden, unspoken desires, dreams, and above all their hope for the unity of the tribes in the vicinity of their existence.

Henceforth creative poetry (not artificially composed stanzas deceptive enough to appear as poetry) moved beyond and above physical existence and emotional need. It became a primary component of life by and in itself. From David's Elegy to Garcia Lorca's elegy for his matador friend; from the eternal *ghazals* by Rumi and Hafiz and Khayyam's rubaiyats (among a nation that as Daniel Ladinsky pointed out poetry is to the [Persian] people what opera is to Italians) to the sonnets by Cesare Pavese and Pablo Neruda; from Milton and Shakespeare to the Bronte sisters, Hughes, and Frost, poets have narrated similar soul-touching universal themes and demands that, as Ben Johnson would say, and Professor Norman Holland would capitalize on, those writings "can please long and please many." Poets, therefore, are not liars even when they may sound contradictory as they narrate certain experiences of their age. Therefore, it is fair to remember that from the beginning of humanity, to varying degrees and in various forms, poetry has been the only art that has presented, discussed, analyzed, emphasized, and expanded "Will to Spirit" (Hegel), "Will to Matter" (Marx), and "Will to Power" (Nietzsche). These three essential schools of human thought have quite logically directed poets to search tirelessly for social justice. Thus, the natural and inevitable presence of reality or phases of real contradictory themes in the work of the same poets have been challenged and even exaggerated by the opponents of poetry.

Do poets contradict themselves over a certain period of time? No, they are too busy living the life they choose so seriously that they deal with a variety of experiences in numerous stages of their lives. And that is why creative poetry is precisely like ripe fruit. When the fruit is ready, it falls from the tree—and not too far from it. But if the poet attempts to speed up this natural process and expects an earlier fall, then the raw product tastes unnatural, unappealing, and goes unnoticed. Creative poetry is the vocal reflection of selected exceptional moments (some good and joyful and some tragic and painful) that a poet has either personally experienced, or has been transformed to that particular zone where others have experienced and shared them with the poet. Therefore, analyzing poetry, using logical criteria and established consistency in beliefs and desires (not style, though) can lead to a dark dead-end frontier. As Oscar Wilde pointed out, "Consistency is the last resort of the unimaginative."

True poets are not the soldiers of the "Moral Majority" or the guardians of certain imposed beliefs and principles. They do not want, or simply cannot be, a Moses living with the burden of leading and protecting a nation. Poets explore and express aspects of life that others do not necessarily find appealing. But they do venture into those frontiers and then return to their ordinary life and depict or report their findings. That is when consistency becomes irrelevant in poetry. Like Alice, poets cannot leave their imagination behind while wandering in unfamiliar, strange wonderlands. They see, they absorb gradually, they assess and compare the new experiences, and when it is ready, the poem becomes that satisfying fruit that can please different tastes. (Consider the observation by William Dunbar: "The state of man dois change and vary,/Now sound, now seik, now blyth, now sary,/Now dansand merry, now like to die;/Timor Mortis conturbat me.) But everyone takes a bite of that fruit in a different manner and therefore the extent of satisfaction varies among different peoples and cultures. In addition to the poet's unique cultural identity, creative poetry defines specific forms of culture in and by itself.

The ability to relate to the culture of a poem and the cultural identity of the same poem is based on a combination of one's knowledge of poetry, extent of creativity, depth of sensitivity, and scope of interest. The culture of a poem is that singular message which has developed through discovery and sophistication of the messenger applying selected terminology and poetic techniques. The cultural identity of a poem, on the other hand, is the reflection of the poet's cultural understanding and development in the environment that is particular to that poet. And then there are poems, cantos, and stanzas that in the most natural manner combine the two entities and leave the reader with the challenge of identifying and separating them. (Omar Khayyam: "A book of Verses underneath the Bough, / A Jug of Wine, a Loaf of Bread—and Thou / Beside me singing in the Wilderness—/ Oh, Wilderness were Paradise enow). A unified definition of the concept of culture is not as significant or critical as the specification of the main traits of a type of culture.

The three types of culture could be identified as universal, national, and regional. (The latter does not always refer to the geographical location but also to the common beliefs that unite a group of people whose domiciles are scattered around the planet.) The core poetic themes not limited to a certain era or a certain country or continent represent the universal culture. But even among the most timeless poems that are in the universal categories there is still a degree of popular appeal and influence that sets most of those poems aside (quite notably this could be observed in the poetry of Andre Gide, George Seferis, Nima Yushij, T. S. Eliot, and Octavio Paz—just to name a few master poets of more recent times).

In "Paradise Lost," for instance, when Adam is replying to Eve, he is addressing a component that develops into a primary aspect of a limitless universal culture: "'Daughter of God and Man, immortal Eve! / For such thou art, from sin and blame entire/No diffident of thee do I dissuade / Thy absence from my sight, but to avoid / Th' attempt itself, though in vain, at least asperses . . . .'" The delicate points stated and implied in these lines do not recognize the human-made boundaries.

On the other hand, in some poems, the primary elements that represent national culture are so internally and fundamentally specific to that culture that, even with the best translation and explanation, those poems make sense at a literal level, but they never quite communicate their true spirit to members of other cultures. As a simple and deep example, examine the following lines from a poem by Maya Angelou: "Too fat to whore, /Too mad to work,/ Searches her dreams for the/Lucky sign and walks bare-handed / Into a den of bureaucrats for her portion./'They don't give me welfare./ I take it.'"

The poems singularly representing the culture of a region are even more complex to those unfamiliar with the details of that culture: details that have been developing, maturing, trimming for decades or centuries as generations living that particular way of life have maintained and preserved them to protect their cultural identity. The exceptional Western movies and books have turned the culture of the American West into a more universally tangible culture for outsiders who have had a love-affair with it. And yet, even those individuals could not completely relate to the nitty-gritty aspects of folk Western poems: "Oh, I've seen them stampede o'er the hills,/when you'd think they'd never stop,/I've seen them run for miles and miles until their leader dropped,/I was foreman on a cowranch—that's the calling of a king;/I'd like to be in Texas for the round-up in the spring." From this example of a relatively new culture in human history, we can move to another poem that might not be singular to a region but the people of a select ancient culture that can relate to it. The stanza that follows is from the poem, "Just as it Was," by Yehuda Amichai: "I gave you a watch instead of / a wedding ring: good and round time, / the ripest fruit/of sleeplessness and forever."

In my final words I wish to include a well-known fact: poetry has always been the backbone of a culture which in turn has kept together nations during the joyful times and disasters. Poets are the guardians of cultural identity. The old belief of "think universally and act locally" cannot have better representatives than poets from various cultures. They strengthen optimism and they glorify their nation as well as the human race. They take pride in who they are and whom they represent. They are certainly the soldiers who bring peoples closer as they keep building bridges among cultures. They may reassess some basic beliefs from time to time; they might be influenced briefly by a major temporal incident; but they remain the sensitive narrators of humanity and the reality of the long, stormy distance peoples have to conquer before getting closer to the rainbow of a better planet for all. History has witnessed that true poets and poetry have been eternally driven and protected beneath the wings of time as they have been courageously enriching and preserving varied dimensions of human culture.

—Aman B. Kay
Augusta, GA
2011/2012

PREFACE

Private

Like an unlisted phone number

Public

Like the life of a deposed monarch

The life of a poet is a maze

As (s)he whispers:

Bury my heart

In the middle of Earth

For hope knows

No human boundaries.

Private or public

Along the edges of tomorrows

The poetry of generations

Will be flying freely

With the wings of time.

WINGS OF TIME

We give our youth
to gain vision and wisdom;
to explore that in a stone-made circle
we leave the centers to live the unknowns.
From the unknowns
—hopeful and blind—
we believe the imposing destiny.

We pass throughout the time-zone
ignoring pain and love until we can stop
and watch time passing.

* * *

The priceless tear of man
was not worth
the dream of freedom and justice?

When did we begin?
Where do we terminate?
From Cyrus and Alexander
to contemporary leaders
and tomorrow-comers

destiny was, is, and will be

a malevolent monster.

Destiny is an ancient and errant vane

flagrantly fooling man

with its promising masks.

Destiny, oh, we did trust it

as it was pleasing us

with its seemingly unending youth!

Yes, we were enchanted

with its murmuring melody

like the calm and sedative sounds

of grandmother's lullaby.

   *   *   *

L O N G . . . .

Longer than man's struggle for justice

we reposed on the time's shoulders

pleasing each other joyfully

believing that our graphic perception

is the ultimate destination for truth!

And we laughed with mirth and blindness

but the ageless monster sneered.

We laughed . . . .; laughed . . . . .

and destiny sneered.

Were we amazed

sinking in another mirage

as destiny was wearing a new, fooling mask

by repeating

a new but old, harmful noise;

our clock was working and we noticed!

Let us be welcomed to the ancient cincture

of silence and endless submission.

The monster is still pleasing,

                fooling,

                              sneering . . . .

And we live, or leave, our conclusions:

Destiny is as ignorant as grudge;

love is as innocent as ignorance.

      * * *

We gave the blood of our youth to destiny

hoping to stop it, mingle with it,

but we lost

as all the gamblers should.

We lost yesterday to gain vision and wisdom;

hence we know

aging is not a disease

like annoying demon of politics.

Destiny is fooling itself!

Like man
It is in search of its identity.
Without a reliable pal at last
Destiny is sinking
and sinkin'
and sin . . . .

Mankind has sunk enough to teach destiny
that the spirit of love
in unending dreams of Gandhi
in Mozart's music
in *Mr. President* of Asturias
in Don Quixote's sagacity
in Picasso's genius
in Becket's bravery
in golden thoughts of Frost
and Langston Hughes
in J. F. K.'s ocean of love
in tomorrow's generations
will survive the machine
and the bitterness of believing:
Past is a present that revives in the future
and memories never die
they resurrect in new forms.

* * *

Like destiny,

I devoted my innovation

to a capricious dream.

She is now a frozen memory

buried under the disgraceful mud of

indifference.

Destiny is as spurious

as my forgotten woman.

With the wings of time

the heavy silences

echo the screech of

the heaviest pain.

And we announce that

destiny is not the solution;

destiny is the eventual enigma.

* * *

We still sit

in presence of destiny

as we duplicate the ancient syllables . . . !

TEMPORAL DOMICILE

In memory of Octavio Paz

"Where are you from?" The strangers have wondered.

"The planet EARTH," I have chuckled.

"Unacquainted and fond

we shall disavow the dispensable boundaries."

* * *

In the streets of Chicago

I have walked with Sandburg.

We have dreamed of a shinier future;

we have anticipated the millennium:

Man is released

   colors are waived

      love is expressed.

Through Sandburg's meditation

I have been heard with other billions:

"I am credulous about the destiny of man,

and I believe more than I can ever prove...."

In Mexico

I learned to breathe your poetry, Octavio!

I danced with a *grupo de bailadores Mexicanos*;

I cheered with the rhapsodies of Margarita;

I sensed the century of solitude

as I believed the presence of Quetzalcoatl!

In Spain, "at five in the afternoon,"
Along with Lorca, I touched the living spirit of Ignacio.
I openly imprecated the ugly afternoon
for taking his bravery and courage away.

New Mexico is where I rediscovered
the secret of love.
A chief gave me a merit feather.
I embraced him with glorious songs
while Sheila repeated with me:
Definitely, "This, Too, is Ours."
This, too, Land of Enchantment, belongs to our planet.
From San Antonio to Big Bend National Park
from Dallas to Port Isabel
from Austin to El Paso
I rode with blue soldiers as we sang:
In Texas the cultures of six flags
are still flying.
Octavio, our nightly prowling
in New York City, Paris, Toronto or Copenhagen
in search of purity, justice and peace,
ignoring the pride and the pain of man

while abandoned in reflection of love
in French Quarter, in Zocalo, or in Montmartre.........
Pour me another scotch or vodka
"All of us are going to die
what else do we know?"*
Salute!

Around the scopes of Olimbos or Persepolis
with Alexander the Great
or the greatest ever ignored, Soorena,
in Polska or Teheran
in Berlin or
Beirut
the graceful commemorations
have been replaced with the ineluctable lamentations.
Marching in the gardens of Lisse
dancing in Munich's bars
singing on Venice's boats
drinking in Stockholm's snow........................

Disregard the places!
Brighten up!
Enjoy your Tecate!
And let's sing with the love's language:

No accent, no fragments, no confusion.

Acapulco or Dublin
Buenos Aires or Tokyo
Tel Aviv or Cairo
with Seferis, Frost, or Darvish;
with Gide, Asturias, or Youshij
with Zeus or Jupiter
we measured love without proper adjectives
we heard the message of Cervantes
lost in our clamorous globe.

Let's leave a shinier planet behind.
Let's teach the coming generations
an eternal anthem which reads:
Our planet, our home
our small cottage of love
where we cry and fight for justice and peace
even if "an unsummoned transparency!"*

"Where are you from?"
"EARTH...................."
Salute!

---

*Lines from Octavio Paz's poem, "The Same Time."

THE BURNING

> "The monster's thoughts were as quick
> as his greed or his claws...."
>
> *Beowulf*

Neither a wandering Jew
Nor a defenseless gypsy
How was I lost in the maze of suffering
In the dark alleys of history
When I began to cry
The powerless tears of dismay
As I gazed over the shoulders of generations
And everlastingly shrank in my mind, in my soul
Watching humanity
Diminishing low, dark, and shameful
In the torturous minutes
Of the eternal Holocaust:
Burning, burning, burning
In the frigid memory of mankind.

Behind the mirror of my loneliness
I sit and fear the return
Of another monster

And the burning

The burning of the defeated cry

Of the silent victims.

MIGRATION

With the gentlest touch
I watch
The migration of love
In the tearful cloudy sky
Of confusion
And surrender.

Life without you
Is an empty bottle of wine
Still tasteful
With no impending cheers.

Miles of silence
Along the dark roads
Of separation
Disturbing the confused birds' songs:
I retire in the halted route
Of your flourishing memories
To begin the purity of life . . .
A warbling chant
Empty as the bottles
Colder, colder,

Yet colder
Than the unkind snowy sense
Of an Alaskan February.

In what mysterious moment
Of living
Did you take our life
With you
When I was still praising

The spring-like comfort
Of your presence.

The glory lines
Of yesterday
Will be
Empty bottles
When the tears
Fill the migration of love
In the sky of stillness.

NEDA'S ETERNAL CALL

Not a goddess from the mazes of mythologies
Nor a famed warrior from the history books
She was a simple witness
With the harmless soul of a butterfly
And the eyes of an eagle:
Oh, those eyes so wide open
So sinless, so vigilant
Witnessing the ultimate, the unconscionable crimes
As life departed her
And she gazed helplessly
At the creatures disguised as humans
Proclaiming their innocence
As merely 'just the excused agents'
Of the Basij-masters whose god knows
But darkness, destruction
And everlasting starvation for fresh brain
Like Zahhak's constantly resurrecting companions*

Her call, her silenced voice will bear witness
While millions of other brave souls
Under the rainbow of hope and liberty

Echo Neda's universal call:

"Let freedom ring!"

Let freedom witness

The fall of the religious leeches

So drowned, so drowned

So drowning still

In the blood of their people.

Hear Neda's call!

Echo Neda's call!

From the seas and the plains

From the hills and the mountains

She is the immortal witness

With defenseless eyes so wide open

Her eternal soul is watching

Her courageous silence is calling.

---

*In Persian mythology book of *The Shahnama (The Book of Kings)*, the evil instrument, Zahhak, became king and each day had to save himself by feeding the brain of two young persons to the two snakes planted on his shoulders by Satan.

REPLY

> "Ringed with the azure world, he stands . . . ."
> —Lord Alfred Tennyson

Fainting hopes

Along the darkest path

Frozen

In the forgotten surrender

Of these formidable

Dead-end dreams.

There

Still

Lives

The tender desire

Of flying

As the eagles' wings leave:

My tall destination

Sunny and ever-living

My songs

The soft verses

Of loving,

Giving,

Dreaming.

Failure

The eagles know

Is not the lost wings . . .

There are piercing eyes

"The wrinkled sea beneath"

And the calm sanctuary

                Of unexplored horizons . . . .

TO ALL THE NEGLECTED GIRLS

Sandras and the Jennifers
Furious, unforgiving
Mumbled a few words
That echoed the darkest cry
Of feminine rage.
I'll hear it
Each time I'm led to walk
Down the bumpy path of memories
Blind, fearful.

I wish my poetry could have a voice:
I've never meant to disregard
The intimidating moment
Of closed eyes and free-spirited lips
And the unleashed hands.
But I was busy
Dreaming, imagining, believing
And the stanzas of my poetry were soundless.

With Jessica, Kim, Gena
Terri, Julie, and Michelles
And a few forgotten names

I was busy connecting the dots.

From the butterfly of my heart
To the roaring gorilla of lust.
The latter lost!
Big time!
And the curse of the women,
Oh, that raging thunderbolt,
Overshadowed my sincere defeat
When the salt water of misunderstanding
Never touched the soul
Of their emotions.

I don't regret
I don't apologize.
There are things better left undiscovered.
There are points better left silent.
There are things I can only love lonely:
In the loneliness of my secluded verses.

THE ANCIENT DREAM

Dream of what mirage leads you apart
Thirsty like the Sahara
Lonely like God.
Let the waves of your hair fly freely
Through the alleys of the homeless wind;
And sleep
The sleep of comfort and security
Under the solitude shoulders of my protection.

Dream of what false spring
Satisfies your thirst for life?
Drink the water of love
From my giant hands
And rest eternally quenched
In my arms:
The Pardis*
Of love and devotion
That Persian palace of peace
The comforting domicile of Kurosh;**
That eternal champion of justice
And devotion;

That solid temple-builder of protection and beliefs.

When you arrive
So lonely, so confused,
Like the moments of awakening
In the purity of dawn
Along the torments of loneliness,
I whisper the magic of your presence
To the roses of sunshine.

Oh, butterfly of freedom!
How did you lose
The joy of the everlasting fly
In the merciless maze
Of fictitious promises and dark hopes?
Oh, ancient woman of always!
Rest under the magical sound of my poetry
And breeze with me
To the long-gone days of glory and truth:

[Climbing the proud stairs
Of Takhte Jamshid***
You were the queen of the empire;
You were the

living dream
When dreams were banished
In the forgotten island
Of loveless existence.]

Oh, lonely butterfly of sadness!
How eagerly, proudly
I want to draw you to me
Like the movements of Mayim, Mayim****.
How child likely
I want to rediscover
The exposed cells of your innocence.

Let the giant hands
Filled with the wine of life and poetry
Nourish the hidden scope
Of your wandering soul.
Let us climb again,
Like the Esther's times,
To the glorious summits of Zagros.*****

Oh, ancient princess of always!
How impeccably eager
I wish to call your name:

Roya, Roya!

My forbidden dream of living and loving.

How am I neglecting life

To be reborn

Beneath the palms of your ever-harvesting breasts.

---

* Paradise
** Cyrus the Great, the founder of the Persian Empire
***Persepolis
****Literary, Water, Water, is the title of a popular dance
*****A mountain range in the Middle East.

ELEGY FOR A WANDERING SOUL

> In loving memory of Milton Arbetter: My teacher,
> my friend, my source of inspiration

The homeless wind whispers
The melody of love and hope
in your name.
And I draw the beauty of the impending days of my life
with the eternal pen of your wisdom
and strength.

Oh, teacher of truth and passion!
Friend of trust and faith!
Your wandering soul,
that fragile butterfly of vision,
above the assuring rainbow of moments
along the path of tomorrows,
is always flying, dancing, observing.
And I see you, proud and hopeful,
murmuring the syllables of history:
Take me to the gathering of
Cyrus, Arthur, and Gandhi
to the feast of human celebration
of peace and harmony.

Call me to the green presence

of eternal spring

in the safety of Urashalem of tranquility.

Lead me to the shining alleys

of concord

and forgiveness.

Oh, wandering soul of inspiration and humility!

search with me—as always—

the mysterious dark corners of our earth

in hope of exploring new dreams,

new melodies, new verses

in the golden shoulders

of the territory of optimism and freedom.

Lead me to the paradise of justice and regards

for the voiceless

and the long forgotten ones.

Oh, living beacon of the warm ocean of memories!

draw me again and again

into the security of your everlasting message

of true anticipation

and beliefs.

Let me rediscover the essence of your life

in the stanzas and cantos

of the simple chant of your optimism
and unending caring words
harmoniously reverberating along with us
as we stare at the waves of life and whisper:
MILTON!

THE SONNET OF DISTANCE

Moments are pebbles of loneliness
Apart from the certainty
Of the rainbow of your flourishing presence
And the stars of memories
Narrating our unconventional union
This unique sanity of ancient wisdom
Reflect the sparks of your eyes
When your laughter,
Sweet, genuine, childlike
Illuminates the depth of the darkness
Of a winter night of doubt and hope

In the far distant alleys of the future
The spirit of my poetry and love
Still awaits your emerging arrival.

LIFE

Dark oceans of silence
Stubborn mountains of differences
Vacant deserts of quarrel
Between us.

Between us
The insensitive tears
And pounding hammer
Of materialistic truth!

Oh . . ., how eager-like, naive,
I still try to conquer
The eternal distances
The lamentable moments of silence
And pain.

From what thread of
Which dying star am I hanging
So desperately, so independently alone?
And how long more will I live
The presence of
My convincing mask

While the indifferent planet of

Hatred and ignorance

Is crushing the shoulders of

My hopeful dreams?

Which unknown dawn

Will open the hidden pathway

To the sunshine of an unconditional love.

THE FALLING BIRD

Alas

The darkest ink

Of the most tormenting spell

Has all but cursed my shattered destiny.

Oh, misfortune owl of shame,

Agony and degrading

How can I turn the pages

Back, back, so far back

To the dawn of the purest love

For an imagined queen

A false symbol of everlasting trust;

An existence of devotion, faithfulness

And joy.

How would I again

Ride so comfortably, so delightfully

Under the wings

Of a lifetime dream:

Her glorious voice

The ever-repeated chant of future

And her soothing security

Leading the dream-path of today and always.

When would I again
Count the melodies
Of the singular stanza
Of her eternal presence
When the shocking dagger of deception
Has violently sliced every cell
Of trust and hope.

How would I, could I . . . .
This real I who loved and glorified her life
With all that might of respect
And decency
And total honest devotion
Can once again
Stare into the past crystal ball
Of our shared, loving union
And hold her
Love her,
And co-breathe the every breath of
Her once enduring companionship.
The hopeless injured bird has fallen
To the lowest point of
The well of destruction

And the sun has forever been
Covered by the dark clouds
Of uncertainty and pain.

Oh, misfortune owl of shame
If I could merely close my ears
To the sneering sound of your
Satanic voice.

THE ELEGY IN AUTUMN

Your oceanic eyes
The enduring extension of my loneliness
Are but
The nest of ever darkness
In crossroads of destiny and shattered dreams.

You bowed to the Grendel of death
In that abandoned mere of life
And I relive the days of the past calendars:
The tears, the laughter, the love
And the dead-end autumn.

THE LOST SOULS

Dream of what endless mirage
Paved your deceptive path
To the Sahara of this unspeakable betrayal?

In what misguided point
Of the fantasy of a false future
Did you lose our imagined oak-like soul
And your expected purity
That the brief joy of
Exploring emptiness of a deceptive creature
Is now the engulfing agony
In every cell of my today, tomorrow,
Always.

I would've moved the mountains for you
I would've drained the oceans for you
I would've celebrated every step
Of your delicate love
In the depth of my honest words and deeds.
But alas you chose the mirage
You chose my eternal pain
While I was still planning

The everlasting sweet moments of our tomorrows.

Where do I hide my shamed self?
How do I ever have dry eyes again?
How would I believe in love:
This seemingly meaningless concept
When I've been so unexpectedly, shamefully betrayed?

I would have sung
The songs of all seasons for you
I would have always traveled
The roads of trust and hope with you.

I would have….
I would have, so candidly….

Oh, yes, I would have moved one mountain
At a time for you
I would have died under the wings of
Your silk-like touch.
I would have sheltered you
Until the late hours of eternity
I would have loved you
Like the colorful butterflies in

A Persian paradise.

How, why did you lose our soul
So shockingly
To that wasted vacant mirage?

TEARS AND CELEBRATION

                    In lasting memory of John Denver

I thought you'd live FOREVER
since you'd come so proud, so strong
from the Rocky Mountain of eternity
from the Country Roads of always
from the neighborhood of Sunshine and all
in the desperate alleys of surrender
and doubt.

I have cried every tear
of pain and loneliness
through the magical sound of your music
your poetry
your contemporary mythology
of human gods.
I have been reborn
in the melodies of your unending love
for man,
for nature,
for tomorrow:
That always lively river

of producing faith.

I've been christened
in the purity of your comforting presence.
You've been the Massih*
on my eternal planet
of hope and dreams;

your songs the ancient Makka**
of my existence.
I've been flying
the spacious frontier of freedom
and those pouring moments
Everlastingly alive moments
of ultimate joy
under the spell of the rhythm
of your global LOVE
scattered so generously
in the skies of uniformity.

Neither lost
in the summits

of your glorious freedom
nor ever trapped by a hidden ego
why were you so impeccably lost
in the merciless bay of evil waves?
Why did you leave behind
miles
and miles
and miles
of a loving heart
so eternally,
so immortally wrapped
in memories of your songs
and your silence?

Where do I search for you?
How could I find you again?
I thought you'd live
until the late hours of eternity.

Like God
and love

and time

I thought you'd be around forever!

And you are

like your presence: Always

in man's daily elegy of struggle

and small victories and joy.

---

*Messiah
**Mecca

COULD WE?

To the rain-soaked roses
Says the young poet:
"The twig of the clouds
Is guarded
By the crystal tears
Of the fish."

Asks the ancient
Wise gardener:
"Could we
One day
Turn our seas
Into another Hiroshima?"

The poet
And the gardener
Together
Cry the tears
Of the fish.

NO MAN'S LAND

The glorious ancient gardens
Have turned into an eternal desert
Paved with the darkest radical ink
And the reddest nation's blood.

The melodies of hope: Inaudible.
The streams of dreams: Rainless.
The eagles of freedom: Aground.
The sun of the future: Negligent.

DARK PASSAGE OF HUMANKIND

Broken,

Shattered,

Lost in disbelief of seeing and denying

When the neo-messenger of aversion

Whispers the demonic melodies

That can resurrect the darkest souls of human's history

That can expand the forces of hatred

And devastation

Once again, like always,

Like the daily rituals

Of all the blood-seeking dictators . . . .

Oh, where's that deserted hole

In which the soul and the body

Can be buried in isolation and comfort?

THAT MONSTROUS GOD

"A thing is not necessarily true because a man dies for it."
—Oscar Wilde

In memory of the global victims of terrorism
and in celebration of the resilient survivors

The egregious components of the synapses of their action

Reproduce their familiar formula:

Bodies and body parts

Smoke, screech, confusion

The horror of disbelief

Running, hoping, gazing

And oh those ancient streams of tears

That have never known rehearsal

Nor the boundaries of race, religion,

man-made territories . . . .

And hence the deceiving calm

And the agonizing silence that can be heard

Throughout the tunnels of the past and future centuries.

Their monstrous god

Who selectively communicates

His scripture of darkness and domination

And the promise of keys of the kingdom

In a private singular language

And meticulously outlines

The joy and lust of eternity with willing virgins

Is so hopelessly powerless

So powerlessly hopeless

So eternally revengeful

That the blood of the old and the young

Flourishes his straw kingdom.

HENCE THE SEASON OF LIFE

In what corner
Of this abandoned, yellow garden of tears
Would I search
The lost innocence
Of belief and trust

I, I—that gullible child
Away from the ancient alleys
Coping with the harsh neighborhoods
Regions filled with metal and brutality
Still awaiting the dawn
Of truthful songs
The assuring melodies of
The impending spring
In the far away horizons
In mirage-like distances

Falling leaves . . .
Falling tears . . .
The path of life
Is filled with piled up dry leaves
Like the throat of my poetry

So unjustly betrayed
So unexpectedly torn

The gullible child
Is still searching, hoping
As he stares into the
Cloudy skies of calendars
And hums the chant
Of future promises

Look up and remember
The sunrise in Jerusalem,
The rainbow in Genoa,
The butterflies in Victoria Island,
The creative whispers in Stratford-upon-Avon,
The unending arrival
Of the flowing Mississippi's waves

Lost, betrayed
Agonized and raged
The child is still remembering
The impending years
Away from the yellow garden
As he is setting his wings free

In green passage of believing

And trusting

And hence the season of life:

The arriving spring

Of hope and peace.

THE FORBIDDEN LAND

The glorious gardens of that ancient land
Have turned into an eternal Lut*
Paved with the darkest radical turbans
And the reddest nation's blood.

The melodies of hope: Irrelevant.
The streams of dreams: Running dry.
The eagles of freedom: Aground.
The sun of the future: Narcissist.

---

*Kavir-e Lut is the largest pit inside the Iranian plateau

THE BROKEN SPIRIT

> "When sorrows come, they come not
> in single spies, but in battalions."
> —William Shakespeare

There's a forceful volcano of rage

and a pounding sound of a stormy disbelief

That lingers over the seconds, minutes, hours

Of this no longer desired life

As I hide the stream of tears

In the veins of a lost, shocked, destroyed life.

How will I meet the floating, reckless seasons

How will I ever remember

the joy of a true laughter

When wavelike I trusted love

Pressed with all the honesty and sincerity

With the foolish, misguided heart of

Lear and Othello.

How will I ever learn to face

the rising sun again,

Oh, that glorious moments after dawn,

In this eternal darkness of agony

When the dreamed angel of my life

Was diminished low, irrelevant
to the destructive spirit
Of a shameful creature
So full and made of nothing
But empty existence and ever dominating
Face of humiliation and shame.

They say, life will go on
And like the persistent waves
Of ocean of life
Nothing will ever alter.
To the suns of yesterdays
To the moons of decent nights
To the stars of hope and promises
The poetry of my blood and heart
Merely whispers the colors of love:
Greens, purples, reds
Oh, can I reverse just a few minutes,
Beg you sincerely,
Just a few misguiding minutes
of a past tragedy
in my own palace,
in my presence,
(the pains of eternity cannot verbalize

this pain of disbelief)
To live a future of
Yesterdays, those comforting, glorious melodies
When I celebrated her arrival
When I trusted the moments of loving, sharing
And believing.
Believing in her!
How does a dream-like queen
Diminishes to the lowest point
Of a capricious irrelevance.

The shattered pieces will never be
assembled back together
even with the divine hands of hope
or the soothing promising voice of comfort.
And one can only cry the pointless
Egregious tears of disbelief
And wonders how a dream-like existence
Can deprive you from a future of endless possibilities.

Oh, what it would've been
All that it could've been.

THESE CHERISHED SOULS

> To my beloved friend, Debra

Alongside this temporal rocky path

This unfaithful, selfish, immortal passage

We, the trusting sojourners,

Smile the routine agonies and pain away

And erase the day's heartache and disappointment

With the power of acceptance and whispers of hope.

We, the ephemeral inhabitants,

Who never truly left

The amusement and transition of wilderness,

We, who never trusted the past

To build the future on our disbeliefs and confusion,

We, the eternal silent observers,

We, the patient souls of humanity

And divine eternity,

We lived the memorable moments,

The holy presence of time

In the vast space of love and dreams.

Errors, yes, we, the transient souls,

Repeated the never-admitting-errors.

And we left the evidence,

The dark traces in history:

The forced conversions, the Inquisition,
The Wounded Knees, the Holocaust, the Nine-Eleven . . . .
We, the visitors, cried our voiceless screams
In the midst of uncertainty and conflicting beliefs
In this crowded corridor of true mourners
And some misguided believers.

And we shall meet again, my partner, my beloved friend,
My trusted, cherished soul:
Not denied "The Promised Land"
Not neglected for human errors, shortcomings
But for the glory of the sacred moments
The memories and the concrete touches left behind.

The ending chapter
Shall echo the opening lines of a future of unity:
A future not tragic, not lamentable, not insignificant
But a future shared in dignity
And joy, and painless comfort.

We, you and I,
The everlastingly trusting souls,
Will fly eagle-like, proud and observant,
Liberated, joyous, grief-free

As we, from beyond the frontiers,
Soothe the pain of the mourners
Who now value the candid presence of our integrity
Of our good, never departed names,
With the magnificent touch
Of our dust-like souls
Comforting them
Whose liberating days are yet to come.

We, you and I,
Like all other cherished souls,
Shall rejoice on a peaceful day
More glorious, more celebrated
Than the day of our birth.

WHERE ARE YOU?

In the deserted neighborhood of your memories
I'm the last, the last wandering soul
Still thinking about our joyful times
Finding my mate is now my only goal

We traveled roads of happiness
We laughed not worried about tomorrow
You were the light, the path to everything
I never thought you'd leave me in sorrow

Under the pouring rain of a late spring
Or when autumn leaves flew away
With the heat of summer or winter air
You were the one who showed me the loving way

> In what part of this world will I find you again
> Light of my life, my one and only soul mate
> I cry blue tears of pain as I wonder why
> I arrived in the wilderness of your love sadly so late

I never imagined my life without you on my side
You were the hope and joy—my only green season
Traveled the past to conquer the present with you

I'll remember the future with you—my life's only reason

I'll send melodies of love with the wings of a breeze
I'll walk rocky roads whispering your name
I am lost and lonely living just a half life
Let people laugh at me; in love there's no shame

In the deserted neighborhood of your memories
Who am I but a determined fateful resident?
Still dreaming, waiting, for your second return
The world can sing my song even if I'm so different

      In what part of this world will I find you again
      Light of my life, my one and only soul mate
      I cry blue tears of pain as I wonder why
      I arrived in the wilderness of your love sadly so late

THE SONG OF ALWAYS

Beneath the rainbow of your enduring love
I flew the blue skies of hope and constant delight;
Along with my Lord you've been my savior
The sole way to heavens' everlasting light

I sang the song of immortal joy and content
Under the red and white stripes and fifty glorious stars
While you rested in my sincere loving arms
Keeping the pain and agony so gracefully afar

That deceiving figure is no splendor in the grass
Fooled you all the way to the mirage of goodbye
You left and took my life on the highway of departure
No shred of hope left for a bird that cannot fly

> I would've whispered the song of always for you
> I would've cherished every breath of life with you
> I would've drained all the oceans for you
> I would've moved all the mountains for you

The empty moments and hurtful hours of this life
Recite the elegy of a lost soul so painfully away
The mirror of yesterday is shattered and lost

It is just the sound of tears and agony all day

The drums of harmony and innocent trust
Are silent and forgotten like the verses of the past
Will our love ever resurrect when you awake
From this nightmare that shouldn't long last

I watch the calendar, the breezing seasons
I long for the melodies of your rainbow
Will you fly back from this deceptive sojourn?
Will you return and allow the song of always aglow

> I would've whispered the song of always for you
> I would've cherished every breath of life with you
> I would've drained all the oceans for you
> I would've moved all the mountains for you

THAT THING

What's that mobile, that invisible thing

Which has been maneuvering

So independently

Within the heart, mind, soul,

Creeping through the blood?

That thing that's closer than every breath

And far, like the never-coming Godot,

Or the dream of eternity.

It's that thing

Restlessly

Making the existence

Always, always lonely

Even in the center

Of a throng of noise and movement.

Oh, if only this loneliness,

So persistently present

In every moment,

In every dreadful second of every day,

Could scream

Freely, fearlessly.

If only this never-fading thing . . . .

Tears never betray

When no one can ever see, comprehend

That hurtful, ominous presence

Of this soul-eating thing

Within . . . .

SONGS BORN TO THE EARTH-MOMENTS

1

Dictionaries of various languages

Cannot explain,

The wisest of each tribe cannot expound

This blind, mad love

Echoed in the melodies of devoted waves

As they recite their singular sonnet

For the furtive shore

And, too, that untiring terrestrial rotation

Hallowing the sun.

2

To the corn poppies

Just so baptized by the relentless rain

He said, "The clouds' twig is guarded

By the waterfall tears of the fish."

Nodding, sneering

The ancient, silent gardener murmured,

"The oceans, too, will be the Hiroshimas

Of the impending darkness."

3

That lively, graceful, optimistic

Stable green leave,

Proud, assured in the paradise of spring

Merely believing in vastness of eternity . . . .

Now the agonizing confusion,

The pain of chasing the wind

In the yellow days of

The apathetic autumn.

Alas, the memory of that green leave.

4

She was drowned

At last

In the lamentable, agonizing pool of sorrows.

Oh, just the depth of knowledge

She scattered;

The waves of pain she left behind

And the lies

The deception of lies

She did not choose to live.

5

Crucified by the golden words;

Lost in the silent darkness of loneliness

He slept under the security of

The lullaby of the stars

The moon rocking his cradle:

The cradle made of jasmines and roses.

The final nails of surrender and acceptance

Shed the blood of truthfulness

In the confessional of deserting calendars:

Dust to dust

An eye for an eye

What else can tomorrows hold?

6

The ancient belief reiterates:

Rain on a sunny day

Is the nature's message:

She-wolves giving birth to cubs . . . .

The communal howls

Echo stronger, more vicious

Along the shameless global territories

And the deaf, voiceless preys

Anywhere, everywhere

Are optimistically attempting

To keep the wolf from the door!

7

Deception: Her existence;

Betrayal: Her religion.

Lies: Her daily resurrection.

The mirrors hide themselves

From her shameless gaze

And the giant famished waves

Lust after her . . . .

She contaminates the world

—though named for a flower!

And the clocks and watches

Gladly long to venture forward

In celebration

Of her glorious eternal absence.

8

Without ya

The pigeons of memories

Have forgotten

The silent chanting rhythm of flying

The compassionate rhyme of loving.

Without ya

The frozen moments

Perceive no sun

No fire

No scripture for living

In the depth of the Southern plains:

Where he awaits

Your promising return.

9

The frank eyes

Are locked in a sudden genuine moment

Of an unexpected,

Never-to-be-explained connection.

They move on

Farther and further

And live the imposed life . . . .

That instant, mysterious connection

Survives in the reluctant reality

Of that moment

And they wonder

How they might have wandered

Along a unified path of future

If only they could've allowed

That genuine moment determine

Their hand-in-hand journey.

10

The sun's alarm

At the resurrection of dawn

Your blossoming smile so immortal

And my reassuring calendar:

The breakfast table

And the pleasing aroma

Of the baked bread and fresh coffee

And life at its most precious point:

The simplicity of the simplest joys:

And, oh, the calm celebration of living
                          And loving.

THE DIVINE AMBASSADOR
OF ETERNAL RAINBOWS

In immortal memory of Peggy Z. Lynch

Tears

I cannot hide

Sorrow

I cannot deny

Memories

I cannot forget

Your voice

I cannot disregard

Your smile

I cannot replace

A handkerchief

Vast as Texas

Cannot erase

The cloudy sky

Of my sufferings

An umbrella

As endless

As your

Genuine love
For all beings
Cannot shield
My trembling soul
And aching veins

You the backbone
Of humanity
For humanity
You the immortal
Poet of past and
Tomorrows and beyond
You the divine
The eternal ambassador
Of blooming rainbows

In a world
So foolishly lost
So selfishly
So hopelessly
So painfully
Divided and confused
You defined
The melodies

Of love
And forgiveness
You
The scripture
Of unity and harmony
Understanding
And loving
For love's sake
You who could
Walk on water and fire
To rescue humanity

You
With your continents
Of love and compassion
You for being
You
And no one else

Trapped in this
Vacant peninsula
Of existence
Only the voice
And smile

Of your

Constant giving

And caring

Elevates the colors

Of eternal rainbows

So firm

So real

So eventual

So poetic

So Peggy

Hear the echo

Of tears

And celebrations

Hear the ambassador

Watch the ambassador

Smiling

Watching

Expecting

Deserving

Living

Beneath and above

The flourishing

Rainbows of always

THAT DREAM THAT DREAMS

> "I Have a Dream . . ."
> —Dr. Martin Luther King, Jr.

A thought

Unimaginable

Like climbing the Demavand*

Without the guidance of the Simurgh!**

The utopia of hope

The pyramid of achieving vision

And all that is, will be possible

Could've imagined it in total darkness.

A thought

A belief

A never-fading dream

Redirected the ancient unpaved road

And a nation

A humanity was reborn

While the Last Supper of constant imagining

And trying

And still believing

Fed the minds and souls

So desperately

So unexpectedly
Harmonized and hopeful.

That thought,
That belief
That singular Dream
Shined and never set
With all the clouds of hatred and ignorance
Blocking its nourishing truth.

Merely an "Impossible Dream"
Still hoping
Fighting
Committing
Beyond the borders
Above the mountains
In street corners
In languages, dialects
Accents
With colors
And flags.

That singular Dream
Is still

Fighting
For the salvation
Of human soul
The Dream is still
Dreaming . . . .

---
*The highest peak of the Elburz Mountains.
**A mythological, powerful female bird that symbolizes protection for the defenseless beings and a zest for life.

For Wade Joseph Smith

Across from the palms of the impending years
may I heed the reflection of your voice:
Love is still my safest pillow
when I rest in the darkness of my solitude;
when I dream in the mazes of the next century.

May you write, Wade Joseph,
with your durable marker
on the skies of all the neighborhoods
on the mountains of earthy zones
on the waves of all the seasons:
Love is still my safest pillow.

May you whisper your message
to the traveling winds,
winds to the butterflies,
and butterflies to the blossoms
as they scatter the alphabets of their hopes
with the wings of universal rainbows.

May you stand tall and still
and sing through the throats of flying birds:

Where man is suffering
my heart is jailed
behind the bars of pain and disappointment.

In 1986 in 24 languages I can be crying:
Who invented the boundaries?
Who placed selfishness above love?
Who stabbed me in the back
While collecting seeds
 for a caring planet?

In 1986 in some languages
love is still forbidden,
for the ruling minds
are ignoring our hearts.

In 1+9+8+6 years
I hope you don't have to announce:
We missed the chance of reaching and believing;
we didn't open the green gates of love's forest.

Wade Joseph,
in 24 years
I wish you don't cry any more:

In the climax of man's blind pride and ignorance
exists the fear of crushing
and being forgotten
like the pages of history
P R O W L I N G
throughout the dead-end alleys of darkness.

In 1986
some days are unkind repetition of surrender
and the moonshine nights
are the unperceived routes
leading you into the options of playing
with the chains of stars
and crying with their memories.

In 1986
moments are our mirrors,
days are our narrators,
and weeks are the reverberates
of our star-crossed compromises.

In 2030
I wish you, Wade Joseph,

don't have to repeat:

Where

be the shore of justice?

Who will be my sound companion

in a world of mistrust and misunderstanding?

In 2030

I wish you burn

THE MONOTONOUS CHANT

OF THE IMPENDING YEARS

EPILOGUE

If the languages of the world

Could just shut up

Eyes and tears

Smiles and silence

Hope and dreams

Visual touch

And universal trust

Could somehow

Unify this disturbed planet

This collective domicile

Beneath the rainbows

Of time

Dignity

The splendor of

Reaching out

Traveling the unending miles

Of the wandering souls

In the paths of history

If languages could kindly

Shut up

And listen

With ears of reconciliation

Perhaps the oceans could be part

A renewed wilderness

Of unity and hope

Could see

The exodus of compassion

From the hateful hearts.

If the languages . . . .

ABOUT THE POET

Dr. Aman B. Kay was a writer-in-residence and anchor for National Iranian Radio and Television and the youngest recipient of the most prestigious national Iranian literary award for his third book. By the mid-1970s, convinced that his ancient homeland was headed for a drastic change, he immigrated to the United States, arriving in Texas where he became a reborn Texan. Over the following years, he received his graduate degrees and educational licenses from different universities in Texas and New Mexico.

For more than four decades, he has taught British, American, and world literature along with AP English and education courses and contemporary American genre novels at secondary schools and universities. His poetry and prose have been published on three continents in several languages. He has received several writing awards, and he regularly delivers presentations at major universities and civic centers primarily in the United States. He has been included in a number of Who's Who publications since 1992 including the 2009 volume of *Who's Who in the World*.

In addition to reading and writing, Aman enjoys jogging/walking and playing tennis regularly. He has a love affair with quality movies and sports, and he especially spends plenty of time following the NFL, NBA, soccer games, and international tennis matches. Currently he is working on several book-length manuscripts and is teaching college English courses.

Made in the USA
Charleston, SC
10 December 2012